Rescue Dogs

The Essential Guide

ROB DUFFY SERIES EDITOR

Published in Great Britain in 2019 by
need2know
Remus House
Coltsfoot Drive
Peterborough
PE2 9BF
Telephone 01733 898103
www.need2knowbooks.co.uk

Contents

Introduction

Owning and looking after a dog is something that gives millions of people and dogs a great deal of pleasure when taken seriously. Although dogs are fun, taking responsibility for one is a lifetime commitment which some people just aren't up to. Sadly, it seems that in today's throwaway society, canine companions often get left on the scrapheap. Worse, before they get there, they are sometimes treated cruelly and inhumanely. The phrase "you wouldn't treat a dog that way" has as much resonance today as it ever has had.

This sad state of affairs is reaching serious proportions in some Western countries. In the famously dog-loving United Kingdom, for instance, the Royal Society for the Protection of Animals (RSPCA) receives reports of cruelty on its emergency hotline every 30 seconds. Fortunately, organisations such as the RSPCA and its counterparts in other countries are well prepared to do something about this. Tighter laws over recent years mean that no dog should be left to suffer for long. Once an animal protection agency steps in, this changes the outlook for both vulnerable dogs and their potential new owners.

Many dog lovers prefer rescue dogs to any others. Specially bred and sold breeds usually cater to a specific market; this can sometimes make dogs more like objects than living creatures. People don't take on rescue dogs to make a profit, they do it out of love. Stepping in after the first steps to recovery have been taken can be a very rewarding experience. These dogs are often looking for someone to love and trust, and will repay those two qualities many times over. With the right attitude, commitment and environment, this is a challenge any real dog lover will relish.

Rescue dogs have their issues, of course. Dogs are sensitive, intelligent creatures who react very strongly to human contact. Just like humans, dogs are also individuals. They have their own personalities, and no two set of circumstances will be the same. Getting to know your rescue dog may take a lifetime, and also be the best thing you ever do. Many people who take on a rescue dog would never consider going to a breeder again.

If you're thinking about getting a rescue dog, this book is for you. Here you'll find tips from the experts to help you avoid common mistakes which other types of dog owners probably won't need to think about. From physical to mental and emotional care, there are many ways you can prepare yourself and develop as a dog owner. Once you've read this guide, you'll have the confidence to take on a rescue dog. You'll also have a handy set of expert tips to prepare you for anything. It's not all hard work, more of a great adventure. Good luck!

1

Owning a Dog

I n order to be of the best use to your rescue dog, you need to be prepared. With that in mind, here are a few basics to bear in mind. Ideally, you should consider these before taking the decision to buy or take care of a dog. At the end of the day, they rely on you to do the right thing when the time comes.

Of course, you are not expected to do everything yourself. In most situations, the vet will be the person to properly fix or remedy your dog's injury or illness, however minor. With that in mind, the following should be of comfort in any situation:

A Vet's Obligation

Legally, all veterinary surgeons are obliged to treat any dog, even if it does not belong to their client. All vets **must** offer an out of hours contact for emergencies. To find a vet in an emergency, do your research early. Go online and see what's available in your area. Don't wait until the time comes and you're already in an emergency.

Try to always use the number listed instead of one saved in your phone in case the contact number for emergencies has changed. **Always have your vet's number handy.**

Safety First

It may not always be possible to help your dog. While this might not seem like a positive way to prepare, it should be borne in mind. There may be situations where doing nothing might be the best course of action. It is important to take a breath and consider the consequences of any actions you might take. Rushing in might not be the right way to prove you love your dog.

Think about the following things:

- Will you put your own safety at risk? You are no help to your dog if you yourself get injured, even temporarily. Remember, your dog relies on you in the long term. His or her health is dependent on yours. Ask yourself if there is a likelihood you will suffer injury, say from passing traffic, being swept away by water or even drowning.

- Will your added presence to the situation put your dog or other people at increased risk? Ask yourself whether standing back and offering to help might be a better solution.

There may be situations where doing nothing might be the best course of action. It is important to take a breath and consider the consequences of any actions you might take.

- Do you need to call the emergency services? While it might be tempting to think about your dog first, there might be a situation which requires attention immediately. Obvious examples are a road traffic collision, railway accident or burning building. Ask yourself if the emergency services shouldn't be involved as soon as possible.

- Are you calm enough to take action? It is vital to remember that your dog will react to the signals you send it. This is the case at all times, but is especially true in situations involving injury and or illness. Your dog will probably be in pain, which will frighten it. If it detects any worry or anxiety in your voice or on your face, this will make everything worse. Ask yourself if you feel in control of your own emotions.

By taking these things into consideration, you have already taken the first step in helping your dog, whether he or she is injured or feeling ill. Dogs have much faster heart rates than humans at the best of times. Calming the situation down will only protect them, and yourself, from any unnecessary discomfort.

First Aid Kit

As being prepared to take the right action is a vital part of giving first aid to your dog, you will find it a great help to have a first aid kit ready. By itemising what is in it, and how to use everything, you will feel more confident if and when the time comes to give first aid. This in turn will help you keep calm, a feeling which you will pass on to your dog.

With a good first aid kit, you will be able to take the right first steps in getting your dog better. Whether this is just in preparation for a visit to the vet, or a permanent solution, the right kit is a huge help. Here are the basics of what you should have at hand, and be confident in using:

- a roll of self-adhesive or crepe bandages (5cm width)

- conforming / open-weave bandages (2.5cm width)

- non-adhesive absorbent dressings (5cm x 5cm) to cover open wounds

- surgical sticky tape

- a box of cotton wool

- a box of sterile absorbent gauze

- blunt ended scissors, preferably curved

- a thick towel

- thermometer
- foil blankot
- disposable, sterile gloves
- saline eye or wound washes
- tweezers
- washing soda crystals
- an Elizabethan collar

An Elizabethan collar has many names, including buster collar, pet cone and E-collar. Light-hearted names include pet lamp-shade and dog-saver. These collars may look strange, but they prevent your dog from doing what it does naturally – paw and scratch itself. As these collars protect the head, this means your dog won't be able to scratch its eyes, ears, nose or mouth. If any of these areas is infected or injured, it's vital that they are left alone once treated.

Although your dog will not like wearing one, practice putting one on while it's healthy and happy. That way it won't mind so much when it has to wear one for real. You might even decide to give your dog a reward for not struggling when you put its collar on.

2

Thinking About Adopting a Rescue Dog

When you take on a rescue dog, you adopt it. The word is carefully chosen, as going through with this is very much like adopting a child. You are accepting the responsibility of taking on a life which began in someone else's home. It is now your job to make your own home welcoming to its new family member. To qualify as a rescue dog adopter, the authorities will have to be convinced you'll do a good job. When they are, you've already passed the first test, so you can be proud of yourself. Not everybody gets to adopt a child, and neither does everyone get to adopt a rescue dog.

It's probably best to approach adopting a rescue dog for the right reason. That reason is that it's best for the dog. Although you might be doing society a favour, that's really irrelevant. If you approach the situation expecting some sort of civic award, you should probably devote your time and effort elsewhere. Dog re-homing organisations will want assurances that you have the time and facilities to look after your rescue dog properly, from the short to the long term. These animals have already had enough upset in their lives, and need a reliable place to call home.

Of course, people buying from a breeder or other private source can make their own choices according to their conscience. Adopting and re-homing a rescue dog is different; in fact, it's often due to irresponsible or incapable owners that dogs need rescuing.

With that said, the commitments you should be able to make are perfectly reasonable. If you're thinking about adopting a rescue dog, here are some basic things you should already be expecting. Obviously, a responsible dog re-homing charity or other organisation will ask you questions along these lines.

Dog re-homing organisations will want assurances that you have the time and facilities to look after your rescue dog properly, from the short to the long-term.

Minimum Requirements

When you go to a dog adoption agency, the people there will need to ascertain that you and your home will provide the right level of care for a rescue dog. Some people go home disappointed that they did not meet the agencies' criteria; but this is for very good reasons. Housing a rescue dog is really its last chance of a decent life. Animal charities in fact have dogs destroyed rather than send them on to a sub-standard home environment. While this sounds dramatic, in fact the things you should be able to offer a rescue dog are perfectly common sense.

Time

One of the most important things you can give your rescue dog is time. As a rule of thumb, rescue dog adoption and re-homing agencies will want to know your pet won't be alone for more than **four hours at a time**. Being close to open space for exercise is only useful if your dog actually has access to it. That means having someone around to take her or him out through the day. People have been refused adoptions because they are out at work all day. Having one walk in the morning and another at night may not be enough.

Dogs feel stressed when they are left alone in a building they can't get out of. They also feel abandoned by their owners when they walk out the door, which causes them huge anxiety. Any young dog will feel these stresses, regardless of their start in life. Bearing in mind that your rescue dog hasn't had a good time of things so far, the more time you spend with her or him the better.

Of course, as a responsible pet owner, you'll want the best for your rescue dog. There are other practical considerations as well, however, which could affect your home life. If you can't commit to having someone around your home with your rescue dog, it may cause itself and your home damage. There is technology available to keep an eye on pets through the day, but that doesn't help the animal itself. Watching your rescue dog become upset from afar doesn't really help the situation, certainly not for your dog.

A four hour time period between exercise and contact with people and animals is accepted as being long enough. Your dog will probably feel like a nap, and hopefully be in a quiet and comfortable environment when it wakes up. As long as she or he knows you won't be long in coming home, all will be well.

Experience

It might not always be a good idea to have a rescue dog as your first pet. Generally speaking, having some experience and knowledge of owning a dog is a huge advantage. Any dog facing a new environment will experience the same sort of stresses, but a rescue dog could be more sensitive than most to change. With this in mind, the more help you can give it, the better. Practicalities like having enough space, so you can separate your pet from other family members, take some working out. Even being strong enough to give commands is something not everyone can do easily.

There is a lot of help available, including online, which may help you in times of need. However, being able to step away from a situation to log onto your laptop may not be possible. Remember, your rescue dog will be looking to you for answers, and it's up to you to provide them, quickly. Having prior experience of looking after any kind of animal might be preferable to none at all.

The charity or other agency you go to will have its own criteria relating to experience. They may think that a particular rescue dog is calm and placid enough not to cause too many problems. On the other hand, the agency will be looking for experienced dog owners to look after some of their rescued animals. Having experience of looking after a dog will certainly increase your chances of coming away with the pet you want.

Resources

Although it might sound harsh, pets cost money. They need feeding properly, insuring and looking after in all sorts of circumstances. There are foods which you shouldn't feed dogs, for example, so their food requirements can be quite specific. (See our section on *Substances Poisonous to Dogs*). Bearing in mind you could have a rescue dog at home for at least a decade, this is a real commitment. Some breeds of dog are cheaper to own than others, largely because they eat less, but insurance is still essential, as is the possibility of accident, illness and injury.

Dogs also need exercising. This is good for their mental well-being as well as essential for their physical health. Depending on the breed and size of your rescue dog, you may need to have access to suitable areas nearby. These could be open fields, woods, or specially laid out dog walking paths and areas. As well as the time (discussed above), you yourself may need to be physically fit enough to exercise your dog. Of course, many people have dogs for this reason; exercising their pets keeps them physically fit as well.

The rescue agency will also assess whether you and your home set up is likely to be a healthy environment for a particular rescue dog. They will ask about the size and layout of your home, how many people live in it, and of what ages. These are not interrogations; however, answering honestly will help the dog agency make a choice. The sad fact is that some people want dogs for reasons other than the healthy and happiness of the animal. Asking you, and maybe your family, questions will give them confidence in you.

FAQs about Rescue Dogs

People worry about whether adopting a rescue dog is right for them. Dealing directly with breeders means you can have a dog from a very young age, of the breed you want, and without any previous history. That may have its advantages, depending on what you're looking for. On the other hand, no two dogs are the same, whatever their lineage and price tag. You will be able to influence some parts of your dog's life, but not its personality. This is worth remembering when buying any dog. Here are some FAQs and their answers regarding rescue dogs:

Are rescue dogs cheaper?

Yes, at least initially. In fact, some rescue dogs will be let out for adoption by charities for no fee at all, if they think you are right for the dog. Even with a fee, paying for a rescue dog will on average be about 90% cheaper than one from a breeder. Of course, looking after a dog for life involves exactly the same costs wherever the animal came from.

Are rescue dogs safe?

There is no simple answer to this question. Statistically, there is no reason to suggest any particular rescue dog will be more or less dangerous than one bought from a breeder. What you can be sure of is that a dog known to be dangerous will never be let out for adoption. Ask the right questions of the dog shelter, take sensible precautions, and get to know your dog. If you see any behaviour which disturbs you, just return it to the shelter.

Are rescue dogs loyal?

The general answer to this is, yes. Some adopters worry that a rescue dog will pine for its previous owners; research and experience show this is not the case. Dogs adapt to their new environment and family very quickly, if allowed to.

Are rescue dogs hard to train?

Again, one size doesn't fit all when it comes to training a dog. When you take on a rescue dog, it is up to you to train it. Any bad behaviours it has learned can be trained out of it. This is looking on the dark side, however; in fact, many rescue dogs have

> Ask the right questions of the dog shelter, take sensible precautions, and get to know your dog. If you see any behaviour which disturbs you, just return it to the shelter.

actually been well trained before their owners had to give them up. This doesn't mean their training should be ignored, however. There is an old saying that any dog is only as good as its owner.

Are rescue dogs good pets?

That's an easy one. Yes. If a dog is happy, healthy and involved in its environment, it will be an excellent pet for as long as you have it. While rescue dogs quickly forget their past, they do like to make up for lost time. That's an excellent opportunity for you as an adopter to forge strong, long lasting bonds with your pet.

3

Welcoming your Rescue Dog

Having been accepted as a good choice to adopt a rescue dog, you need to hit the ground running. The first 30 days with your now pet are vital to its chances of a healthy, happy life in your home. It can't be stressed enough that getting this early period right will make all the difference in the world, both for your new pet and your home life. This precious time establishes routines and behaviours which will hopefully last your dog a lifetime, and help her or him settle into your home as an established family member. It will also give you the confidence that you've made the right choice, and make you optimistic for the future. The following steps are tried and trusted to achieve just that.

Before Bringing Your Dog Home

The first thing you should do when adopting a rescue dog is to make sure everyone in your home is ready to go ahead. Everybody needs to be on board, and singing from the same hymn sheet, as the saying goes. Your rescue dog will be looking for certainty above all else, and getting the same messages from the new people in its life is vital for this. Dogs will pick up on any negative vibes from family members, so ideally everyone should be as happy as you with your new pet.

- **Language.** From then on, you can make sure everyone literally speaks the same language. Discuss with your family exactly what commands you will be giving your new pet. Learning to talk to your dog is a vital skill to have, and makes things easier for all concerned. There are excellent resources to help with this online. One basic rule to remember is to use your dog's name before giving any command. This, of course, means agreeing a name. A lot of the time, however, a rescue dog will already have a name; in which case, it's important to keep using that.

- **Space.** Before bringing your dog home, you'll need to decide exactly where it can and can't go. You may find it easier to confine your new pet to the kitchen to start with, for example. Remember, it needs to know where it stands in your home, so set boundaries immediately. You may choose to bring your dog inside via one particular door only, such as the kitchen door. As long as you and your family stick to this every time, your dog will be happy. The kitchen is also a good room to choose to begin with, as your dog may have forgotten its house training. *Don't* let your new pet into your living room and then scold it for messing up the carpet.

> Discuss with your family exactly what commands you will be giving your new pet. Learning to talk to your dog is a vital skill to have, and makes things easier for all concerned.

- **Crate Training.** Some dog owners find it best to crate train their new pets. Not all pet owners agree, but it may be suitable to your circumstances. Crate training is an extension of allowing your rescue dog its own space within your home. It also helps with what is called house training, i.e. teaching your pet not to urinate or defecate indoors. Using a crate gives owners more control over this process, and also helps with teething. Those who crate train say that it gives their pets extra security, as they feel safe there at all times. If you are going to use this method of house training, you need to have it set up and ready to go as soon as you bring your dog home.

- **Early Precautions.** For the first few weeks in its new home, your dog will have a lot on her or his mind. There are lots of rules to get used to, as well as the new smells, sights and sounds of the new environment. With this in mind, take precaution in whatever space you give to your dog. If it is to be the kitchen, for instance, tape up any loose wires, and keep any dangerous substances well out of your dog's reach. This includes foods which are harmful to it. You may also need to install child-proof gates if you have small children.

Finally, when you go to pick up your new pet, take its ID tag with you. This should have your contact details on it, and needs to be put in place straight away. It's not unknown for rescue dogs to try to escape during their first journey in a strange vehicle. Also, if your new pet is microchipped, this should be registered immediately. The animal adoption agency may have seen to this, but it's important to check.

Day 1

On the big day itself, make sure you have everything in place for when you bring your rescue dog home. This is the perfect time to introduce your new pet to its home and the routines that come with it. If you are crate training your dog, take this crate with you. Transporting your new pet will be very stressful for it, so don't take any unnecessary risks. For help on moving your dog, check out our section on *Transporting Your Dog Safely*.

When you get your new pet home, introduce it to its new surroundings gently. Use the door you have chosen as your dog's entrance and exit, and bring it into the room it will use first. Give it a chance to have a look – and sniff – around, at its own pace. As you will have prepared the space beforehand, you won't have to chide your new pet for doing something it shouldn't.

- **Check** with the pet adoption agency to see when your dog was last fed, and what its feeding routine is. Stick to this routine for the first few days. It may be best to give your dog a drink of water after its journey in your vehicle. This is a good chance to introduce it to its water bowl. This shouldn't interfere with your pet's feeding routine, however.

The first thing to do is to take your dog to its toilet area. It may want to relieve itself straight away, but might also hit the wrong spot to start with. Don't be too hard on it initially, as it will be stressed from the journey and these new surroundings. You can at least make it obvious where your dog should go to use the toilet. If you are crate training, take it to its crate immediately; of course, you will have used this to transport your dog already.

After your dog is used to its new toilet arrangements, introduce it to things and people gradually. Don't overwhelm it with a huge family welcoming party. This will over-excite and possibly upset the animal, which may cause it to bark, whine, attack or mess on the floor. These are the very last things you want to happen. Make each introduction pleasant and stress free.

- **Children.** If you have children, let them meet their new dog one at a time. Everyone has their own scent, and your dog will need to register each person's individually. There are also behaviours to look out for which are warning signs your new dog may not be happy around your children.

You should then start your new routine immediately. This means toilet training, feeding, exercising, play and quiet time. Make sure any family members are fully on board with this, so that your rescue dog's routine is not disrupted. This will confuse your pet and delay the settling in process. You may need to be strong in the early stages of re-homing a rescue dog. If it helps, use a chew to help your dog settle during quiet time. There may be some chews and / or other toys which the dog is already used to, as provided by the animal agency. If not, choose a toy or other object your new pet can chew on to help it keep calm.

Be as quiet as possible around your new dog for the first day or so. Any extra noise will excite it more than it already is, so anything you can do to introduce calm will help. If you have children, it will be natural for them to be excited to have a new pet. In the very early stages, this may mean keeping them away from your dog during certain times.

The First Few Weeks

From the start of your new pet's second day at home, you can congratulate yourself that you've got the hardest part over. Qualifying for, selecting and adopting a dog are not easily achieved. Then, bringing them home and getting them settled into a routine and new environment is also a major achievement. You could say that you've done all the hard work, so now all you need to do is keep it up. This means sticking to routines, but it also means having patience. Don't expect your rescue dog to be grateful, or even settle down immediately. People who adopt dogs often say their personality takes a few weeks to show through. It takes time for them to gain confidence in their new surroundings.

As well as basic routines like toilet and feeding times, you can gradually introduce new aspects of daily life. At some point, your dog will need to be introduced to other dogs, in your immediate neighbourhood and the parks or paths where it will go for exercise. As a rescue dog, your pet may have had bad experiences with other animals, so it's important to be aware of its reaction to anything new. As well as having patience, this means being vigilant at all times.

You don't want your dog to be frightened of other dogs, but neither do you want it to be a bully. Signs of either will be easy to spot if you know what to look for. Again, this is where having experience of owning a dog comes in handy. Some signs to look out for when your dog is with other dogs are these:

You don't want your dog to be frightened of other dogs, but neither do you want it to be a bully. Signs of either will be easy to spot if you know what to look for.

- **Positive signs.** If your dog is happy and relaxed around other dogs, its tail will be up, wagging side to side or even in circles. At play, she or he will bounce around with other dogs, and probably roll over to show off its tummy. Barking is normal during play, but will be high pitched, unlike a warning bark.

- **Warning signs.** If it is frightened, a dog will bring its tail down, or between its back legs. Another sign is that dogs look away from other dogs when they approach, as if pretending not to see them. Other signs are backing away, and barking loudly and deeply. A frightened dog might also yawn and lick its lips.

- **Bullying.** This is important to look out for in rescue dogs; they may have been bullied or been bullies themselves before getting to you. If your dog retreats, and is pursued by another, it's being bullied. Similarly, if it pursues another frightened dog, it's doing the bullying. In both cases, it's time to intervene. This should ideally be done with the cooperation of the other dog owner.

- **Normal play.** Dogs playing together can get boisterous and maybe even noisy. This isn't necessarily a bad sign, so long as no one dog in particular takes the lead all the time. During normal play, dominance will pass between dogs, and they will keep displaying positive signs.

- **Rough play.** Depending on what they're used to, dogs can become overly rough when they play. This may result in the other dog yelping or barking. If the rough dog persists, it may have been trained to do so. It is essential to stop this behaviour quickly.

As a dog owner, you will soon get used to other owners and their pets in your area. Avoid confrontations where possible, but let your rescue dog make its own friends and mistakes. As long as you're close by, this shouldn't get out of hand. Your pet will then look forward to its regular exercise and play sessions, which will build its own confidence as well as the bond between you. As your dog grows, your exercise sessions may well need to get longer. As long as you introduce this gradually, this will seem a natural part of your pet's routine.

First Aid Basics
for your Dog

Giving first aid to any living creature is something which benefits from practice. There are physical and emotional barriers to overcome, something which is best done as quickly as possible. If you can, attend a first aid course with your dog, so that both of you have some idea of what it feels like to be in such a situation. The advantage you have in giving first aid to your own dog is that you are used to each other.

Familiarity can be extremely important in situations where pain and fear are involved, and especially so with dogs. A dog's first instinct when injured or ill may be to attack anything or anyone that comes near it. As a dog owner, hopefully you should have a trusting relationship with your pet, reducing the risks of this happening hugely. Always remember only attempt first aid if you judge it safe to do so.

With that in mind, here are the basics of giving first aid to your dog.

Take Control

The most important thing to remember when giving first aid to your dog is that **you are in charge**. Left to its own devices, your pet might lick its wounds or find somewhere quiet to hide until it feels better. What you are doing is intervening, which brings responsibility. You **must** be ready for the situation, and appear fully confident in what you are about to do, even if you are maybe actually not all that sure.

The important thing is that your dog thinks you know what you're doing. This will help it relax as much as possible given the situation, knowing it's in good hands. As you may well need your dog's cooperation, this is an advantageous position to be in, for both of you.

Of course, some situations will be much easier to handle than others. If you are afraid of blood, for example, you will find it much easier to deal with a sprained ankle. However, it may pay you to have some kind of exercise ready for yourself if you need to face your own fears. Many people find deep breathing exercises useful, for example.

One thing that is certain is that if you panic, you will pass this on to your dog. If you know that certain things are likely to upset you, have something in your locker to help you get over the worst.

> The important thing is that your dog thinks you know what you're doing. This will help it relax as much as possible given the situation, knowing it's in good hands.

Have Your Kit Handy

If your dog takes ill at home, you have many advantages. Firstly, he or she will be in their favourite place, and hence feel as comfortable as possible given the situation. Secondly, you will be well placed to get in touch with the vet, and act accordingly. Thirdly, you will have access to your dog's first aid kit.

If, however, you are out and about with your dog, it will probably not be practicable to take your full first aid kit with you. This may be an excellent idea if you are going hiking in the mountains, where you will have rucksacks to carry your equipment. However, for local walks and exercising, this is not likely to be the case. What you can do, however, is take a few things from your kit with you which might come in handy, such as:

- tweezers
- tick removers
- a clean cloth for wiping eyes or scratches.

Little things such as these can at least keep your dog comfortable until you get home. You can keep them in the same pocket as your clean poo bags.

Pay Attention

Unfortunately, when many people take their dogs for a walk they ignore them. Especially if they are in an area which doesn't require use of a leash, some dog owners or walkers let them go wherever they want. While this might seem like giving your dog freedom to enjoy itself, there are many reasons why it's a bad idea. Even if your dog is within your sight, it can get into trouble in the blink of an eye. Apart from other dogs and dog walkers, there are a thousand smells which will attract your dog's attention at any one time. This may lead them to dash out of your sight before you can stop them.

By paying attention to what your dog is doing, you can quickly see if something is wrong. If it returns to you with a slight limp, it may have stood on something sharp. If it looks a bit worried, it may be in pain of some sort. While it will not want to spoil your fun, you should check out any signs of strange behaviour.

Of course, the better you know your dog, the easier the signs will be to spot that something is wrong. It may just be a tick, for example, which is easily removed if you have your tick remover with you. The point is, the sooner you spot any danger signs, the better position you are in to do something about it.

Making Your Dog Stable

If your dog has suffered a distressing injury, or is feeling particularly unwell, you may need to stabilise it. As dogs are very sensitive creatures, they can become upset easily. This can lead to further injury or worse illness, as the dog panics because of something it doesn't understand.

Even if you are able to deal with the problem yourself, you will find that having techniques to calm and stabilise your dog come in extremely useful. If, on the other hand, you need to wait for, or travel to, a vet, keeping your dog stable can be absolutely vital to its overall health and well-being.

Stabilising your dog might be as simple as producing its favourite snack. As long as this has the effect of calming it down, this is all to the good. For more major interventions, however, you may need other resources.

Safe Restraint

If you need to restrain your dog, you **must** do this carefully. This is to protect yourself as well as your pet. No dog likes to be restrained, as you will know every time you let yours off the leash. There are steps you should take in order to make this process as easy as possible.

- **Light Restraint.** This is the most pleasant type of restraint. This is because it can be done without any physical discomfort whatsoever, and is more like everyday owner – dog behaviour. If your dog is well trained, it will respond to your commands. Sit, down, stay and no should be the basis of any sound training. Tell your dog to sit, and then you will be able to apply its collar, if it's not already wearing it. If you have a dog which requires a harness, apply this unless it will cause further discomfort or distress.

- **Heavy Restraint.** If your dog is distressed, applying heavy restraint will calm it down. Your commands and actions will help it override its instincts, and comply with you. This will take away its panic and desire to flee or fight. There are techniques which your vet can teach you in order to safely practice heavy restraint. This may include using a muzzle, or safely restraining your dog with your arms. **Do not attempt unless you are 100% confident of what you are doing.** Dogs are liable to bite when they are distressed, even if it is their owner.

Once your dog is safely restrained, you will be able to apply first aid yourself, if your vet has advised it. Otherwise, your pet is able to be calmly transported to the veterinary surgery.

5

Choking and Resuscitation

Choking

Choking is one of the most worrying things that can happen to your dog. It will be extremely distressed and frightened, and no doubt so will you. It is, of course, vital not to panic in such a situation. You will need a very calm head in order to act quickly to remove the obstacle. Depending on how long the choking has been happening, you might then need to resuscitate your dog. Both of these steps can be achieved with the right knowledge and attitude on your behalf.

If your dog is showing signs of choking, you will first need to restrain it. As it will already be in a state of panic, any attempt on your part to access its throat will cause it to want to bite you. In other situations, your dog might actually be unconscious. If this is the case, the procedure is slightly different.

Gaining Access

If you have restrained your dog, or if it is unconscious, its mouth may be shut. To open it, put one hand over your dog's muzzle and take hold of its upper jaw with your other hand. This is the safest way of ensuring your dog is not able to bite you, whether it is conscious or not. If it is unconscious and wakes up suddenly, its first instinct may well be to bite.

- Press firmly on your dog's upper lip, so that it is a barrier between your fingers and the dog's teeth. Hold the top teeth firmly and pull upwards, opening your dog's mouth.

- If you can see an object in your dog's throat, pull it out with your free hand.

If you can't see any obstruction, your next step depends on the size of your dog.

- If your dog is small enough for you to lift safely, pick it up carefully by its back legs. Once you have a hold of it, shake it up and down with its head facing the ground. Do this vigorously, and pat it firmly on the back if you can while you're doing it. You're trying to force the choking object out of your dog's throat using gravity movement.

- If your dog is too big to lift up, lie it on its side and try to dislodge the object using pressure on its chest. Put your hand flat on your dog's flank with the heel of your hand just below your dog's ribcage. Push quickly and firmly, downwards and slightly forwards, in a sharp movement. Do this a few times, until the object comes loose. You're trying to use the air in your dog's lungs to force the object forwards and out through its mouth.

If you have restrained your dog, or if it is unconscious, its mouth may be shut. To open it, put one hand over your dog's muzzle and take hold of its upper jaw with your other hand.

- If you cannot dislodge the choking object from your dog's throat, take it to a vet immediately. See our section on *Transporting Your Dog Safely*.

If you do manage to dislodge the object, your dog may start breathing again spontaneously. If it does not, you'll need to resuscitate it.

Resuscitation

One of the most important things you may ever be able to do for your dog is resuscitate it. While this process is something mostly associated with people, in fact it is perfectly possible to carry out on your pet. Acting quickly and appropriately in the right circumstances can quite simply save your dog's life. Of course, no dog owner ever wants to be put in such a situation. If you are, however, it is helpful to remember that the successful steps to resuscitation are literally A, B, C. This stands for Airway, Breathing and Circulation.

ABC and CPR

Another handy acronym to remember when thinking about resuscitating your dog is CPR. This stands for Cardio Pulmonary Resuscitation, and is exactly like that carried out on humans. Basically, if your dog is in serious trouble and has stopped breathing, you can resuscitate it by getting its heart and lungs working properly again. The quicker you are able to do this, as with humans, the less damage is likely to have been done. As long as your pet's brain has not been starved of oxygen for too long, a complete recovery is possible.

Of course, you need to be confident when attempting CPR on your dog. There are classes available which will show you what to look for, and what procedures to carry out. These use canine CPR dummies, which are specially designed to give you an idea of what it feels like to resuscitate your dog.

What dummies cannot replicate, however, is the smell of your dog's breath. Like the shape of its whiskers, you will no doubt be familiar with this. It is details such as these which can tell you if your dog is need of resuscitation.

Airway

If your dog Is Immobile and you cannot rouse it, there is obviously something wrong. In order to check to see if it's breathing, you can look for its ribcage. If you feel or see no movement there, check its muzzle. You will be able to see any signs of breath on its whiskers. If these are still, put your face close to your dog's mouth and nose. You will be able to detect the smell of its breath if it is breathing.

If none of these signs are present, open your dog's mouth gently. Pull its tongue forward out of the way and check inside for any objects in its throat. If you see something, try and remove it with tweezers. **Do not** push any obstructions further down your dog's throat. Pull the tongue all the way out in order to help any object free itself.

Once any obstructions are out of the way, your dog may start to breathe. If it does not, and you are sure there are no obstructions in its throat, you should check for a heartbeat. To do this, put your finger tips under your dog's left leg where it joins its body. You will feel any heart beat through gaps in its ribs. If you feel nothing, you need to start resuscitation quickly.

Breathing

With your dog on its side, lift its nose upwards slightly so that its head tilts backward enough to open its airway completely. Once you've done this, close your dog's mouth completely and blow straight up its nose. This may not seem like the most obvious thing to do, but you'll soon get used to it. Obviously, your dog's nose will be cold and wet, so be ready for that.

Blow hard into the nose for a few seconds. Obviously, the bigger your dog, the more air you will need to inflate its lungs. Be a bit more careful with smaller dogs. Repeat this exercise every few seconds, for 10 times a minute.

Circulation

To help get your dog's heart beating, combine breathing with compression. In between breaths, compress your dog's ribcage enough to press on its heart. Obviously, how hard you do this will depend on your breed of dog. Any compression you give it will help stimulate its heart, so err on the side of caution. You don't want to break any of your dog's ribs.

Try to get a rhythm going between breathing and compression. If you have help with you, this will probably be easier, especially with a larger dog. Ideally, you want to combine a six second breath with at least six heart beats. Of course, this is very much easier said than done. If you've had practice, you'll know better what to feel for and how to go about it.

Aim to compress between a third and a half of your dog's ribcage, into about two thirds of its chest cavity. In the case of small dogs, this will be very easy to achieve. For big breeds, you may have to use your own weight, possibly with one hand over the other. Once you have got into a rhythm of breathing and compression, the job of resuscitation becomes easier.

CPR for Smaller Dogs

If your dog weighs 45 pounds or less, you may find the following CPR techniques easier to carry out.

- Turn your dog onto its back. Kneel down at its head, and bring the head up onto your lap, facing upwards.

- Lead forward and place your hands flat on your dog's ribcage. Clasp your fingers together to make a solid barrier of both hands.

- Press down on the ribcage for two seconds. Release for one second, and repeat. You'll get a feel for how far down to push the ribcage, and counting 1,2 and 3 will help with your rhythm.

- As your dog's muzzle is facing you, you'll be in the perfect position to breathe into its nose. For smaller dogs, this won't take as much breath. If you blow for three seconds, this should easily be enough to inflate your dog's lungs. Eventually, you will feel some resistance, or your dog's chest will rise.

The recommended ratio for CPR is 5 chest compressions to 1 assisted breath.

CPR for Larger Dogs

If your dog weighs over 45 pounds, the technique for administering CPR is slightly different.

- Turn your dog on its side. Kneel down next to it and place the full span of one hand in the middle of your dog's ribcage.

- Push forward with the heel of your hand, compressing the ribcage for two seconds. You may have to adjust your weight to achieve the right amount of compression.

- Release for one second and repeat.

- After 30 seconds (or 10 compressions), start to breathe into your dog's nose. You may have to take very deep breaths yourself to inflate its lungs for 3 seconds. Combine breathing and compressions in a ration of one breath after every five compressions.

Checking for Signs

After a minute, recheck your dog for signs of breathing and heart beat. It is possible that it has started breathing while you were administering CPR. If not, repeat the process 10 times, over 10 minutes. If there is no sign of breathing after this, unfortunately it is unlikely to return.

If you are successful in resuscitating your dog, remember to take it to the veterinary surgery as soon as possible. For help in doing this, see the next chapter of our guide *Transporting Your Dog Safely*.

6

Transporting Your Dog Safely

Applying first aid to your dog is an excellent first step in ensuring its full recovery from illness or injury. In many cases, however, it is just that; a first step. Most of the time, as you will read in this guide, the first aid treatment is completed by a trip to the veterinary surgery. Just as you wouldn't trust yourself to cure your family of many of the ailments described here, so you should entrust the health of your dog to the professionals.

In fact, transporting your dog safely *is* an excellent first aid skill to have generally. You may need to take your dog to many places, not just to the vet's. Dogs are designed to walk and run, not sit or lie down in cars. For this reason, they can become distressed when forced into such a situation. While you know it's for their own good, they don't.

Learning how to get your dog safely from a to b while not under its own steam could serve both you and it well in the future.

Lifting Your Dog

If your dog cannot get into your vehicle because it is injured or unwell, you may have to lift it. How easily this is achieved will depend to a large extent on the size, age and breed of your dog. You know your dog best, and whether or not you will need assistance.

- If you have a small dog, take hold of its collar at the back, and reach round and underneath your dog's torso. Using both hands at the same time, pull forward on the collar and lift with your other hand. Pull your dog towards you, and cradle it against your body.

- If you have a larger dog, bend down with your back straight towards it. Hook one arm underneath its neck, so that its throat is in the angle of your arm. Make sure you're not blocking your dog's windpipe. With your other arm, reach under your dog's stomach and up backwards towards yourself. In one movement, stand up straight and bring your dog towards your chest.

- If you have a very large dog, make sure you can manage its weight on your own. If you can, bend down towards it and reach round its front, so that your dog's chest is in the angle of your arm. With the other, reach round under your dog's tail, so you have its hind quarters between your shoulder and forearm. Bring both your arms together while you stand up straight.

If your dog cannot get into your vehicle because it is injured or unwell, you may have to lift it. How easily this is achieved will depend to a large extent on the size, age and breed of your dog.

Using a Stretcher

If your dog cannot be lifted for whatever reason, you may need to improvise a stretcher to get it to your transport. This can be done with a blanket or a board. If you suspect your dog has a broken back, a flat board is an absolute necessity.

For a blanket stretcher:

- With the blanket stretched out between you and your dog, lean forward towards your dog.

- Slide one hand flat under your dog's shoulder, and the other under its hip.

- When you have enough purchase, either lift or slide your dog backwards onto the blanket.

- When your dog is in place, bring the two sides of the blanket together and lift your dog into your vehicle.

For a board stretcher:

- Find a flat board large and strong enough to cover the area of your dog on its side. How big this is exactly will depend on your dog and the size of your vehicle. Useful examples are ironing boards, table leaves and removable shelves.

- Lie the board between yourself and your dog, with the dog's back towards you.

- Lie two or three strips of strong cloth or other material underneath the board. These will support your dog's torso, between its front and rear legs, so estimate where you should place them to achieve this.

- Lean forward across the board towards your dog. Slide one hand flat under its shoulder, and the other under its hip. Pull towards you, so you either lift or slide your dog onto the middle of the board.

- Bring the lengths of material together over your dog's mid section and tie each one firmly, but not so tight as to affect your dog's breathing or hurt it.

- Once you are satisfied your dog is safely tied to the board, lift it into your vehicle.

Bandaging and Medication

Learning how to apply bandages to your dog can be a superb first aid skill. Bandaging can help support damaged limbs as well as holding dressings in place. A properly applied bandage will help your dog feel safe while its wounds heal. Similarly, learning how to give your dog medication is something that not everyone knows how to do properly, but is an important procedure. As there could be a whole host of reasons why your dog needs to take medication, and they don't like taking it, knowing how to do this safely is an excellent first aid skill.

Bandaging

Of course, veterinary nurses are the experts at applying bandages, and you should take your dog to the veterinary surgery for real professional bandaging, but following the right steps can really help your dog in the meantime. On the other hand, a badly applied bandage can actually do your dog harm.

It is recognised best practice for bandaging to consist of four layers;

- A non adhesive dressing directly touching the skin. This is especially important in the case of bleeds and burns, and is known as the swab layer. This layer **must** be absolutely sterile, and sit on skin which has been thoroughly cleaned.

- On top of the swab layer, a conforming cotton wool bandage is applied to completely cover the swab and surrounding area.

- The third layer is a conforming bandage, which holds the first two firmly in place against the skin.

- Finally, an outer layer of vet wrap or other brand of non-adhesive material completes the bandaging.

Depending on the type of injury your dog has, once bandaging is in place it may be left for varying lengths of time. Open wounds and burns will require bandaging to be checked and changed once a day. This is both to see how the wound is progressing, and to check for any signs of infection. Bandaging which is used to support limbs after sprains etc. can be left in place for longer periods. Your vet will advise you when to come in for a change; this itself can change if the bandaging comes loose, wet, damaged or your dog chews it.

Depending on the type of injury your dog has, once bandaging is in place it may be left for varying lengths of time. Open wounds and burns will require bandaging to be checked and changed once a day.

In the case of your dog's leg, a veterinary nurse will bandage the whole limb. This might seem strange at first, but there are excellent reasons for it. No matter where the wound is, or whether it is internal or external, bandaging needs to be done properly. This is mainly due to blood supply.

- A properly applied bandage will always start from below the wound; this means as far away from the heart as possible.

When applying a bandage, you should bear this in mind. You don't want to wrap bandages too tightly, but they have to be tight enough to keep the layers in place. By starting after the wound, it's easier to judge tension, and it avoids the danger of cutting off blood supply before it gets to the affected area. Working inwards is the best way of ensuring continued blood supply.

If your dog has a bandaged limb, there are ways of checking to see if its blood supply is still healthy. If it is not, you could notice one or more of the following signs:

- A swollen paw or distal limb
- Red or purple skin beyond the bandaged area
- Cold feeling paws or lower legs
- A foul smell coming from the wound
- Your dog repeatedly trying to lick and or chew its wound.

Your dog needs its blood supply to heal its injury, whether that is a bleed, burn, break or sprain. Apart from this basic requirement, bandages wrapped too tightly will be uncomfortable, and may cause numbness. If you notice your dog in any distress after bandaging, inform your vet straight away. When applying bandages yourself, try not to wrap the outer layer too tightly. This is especially important if you are not planning to take your dog to the vet, perhaps because it only has a minor injury. Be careful not to assume that your dog is showing signs of distress purely because of its injury. It could be trying to tell you that its bandages are too tight.

Medication

Dogs can take medication in liquid or pill form, just like humans. Also like humans, dogs generally **do not** like taking their medicine. While human patients don't generally bite the hand that medicates them, dogs sometimes do. You may need to give your dog medicine for a serious injury or illness; or it could be a regular prescription drug for worms. Either way, here are some helpful tips to help the medicine go down:

You will need to apply safe restraint to your dog, using your calming vocal techniques. As you will be administering medications orally, you will not be able to use a muzzle. This may mean you have to keep hold of your dog in continual restraint until you have given it all of its medication.

Liquid Medications

For liquid medications, use a syringe or eye drop applicator with the correct dose. Have this ready before you start working with your dog.

- While continuing to talk comfortingly to your pet, crook your arm under its neck gently. Take care not to block its windpipe.

- Use your other arm to bring your dog close towards you. You can go either under or over its body, then pull inwards. Keep your dog firmly in that position while you administer its medication.

- If you have one, and if you judge it necessary, apply a mouth tie to restrict your dog's jaw movements. Tip your dog's head backward slightly so it's looking above the horizon.

- Insert your finger into the bottom corner of your dog's mouth and pull out its lip slightly. This will form a small pouch.

- Put a few drops of the medication into the pouch and let your dog swallow naturally. Stroke the underside of its throat if you need to help it swallow.

- Repeat until your dog has swallowed the whole dose.

Solid Medications

When administering solid medications such as pills, tablets or capsules, have the right dose ready before you start.

- After safely restraining your dog, keep talking to it and put one hand over its muzzle. With the other, take hold of the upper jaw from above. Use your thumb on one side and your fingers on the other.

- Press your dog's top lip onto its middle to rear teeth, so that your fingers don't touch your dog's teeth or gums. Once you have a firm grip, pull the top jaw upwards.

- When your dog's mouth is fully open, take the pill between the thumb and forefinger of your other hand. Place it carefully deep into your dog's mouth, as far back as you can.

- Rub your dog's throat to stimulate its swallowing reflex. When the pill is swallowed, gently release your dog's top jaw.

8

Dealing with Bleeding

After resuscitation, one of the major ways you can help your dog with first aid is by dealing with bleeding. While this can be traumatic for both your pet and yourself, it is an excellent set of skills to have. Apart from your dog not breathing, nothing signals that its health is in danger than the loss of blood. Although major bleeds are more obviously upsetting initially, even minor ones can be serious if not treated promptly and correctly.

If you are frightened by the sight of blood, it's a good idea to find ways of getting over this. Keep in mind that dogs can bleed for all sorts of reasons. Also, dogs usually have dense fur which soaks up blood. You may have to get to the source of the bleeding to determine what if anything you should do about it. The braver you can be, the better the result for your dog, both in the short term and the long run.

External Bleeding

Apart from the likely distress it will cause, the main reason to stop bleeding as soon as possible is to prevent shock. If your dog loses enough blood, its nervous system will go into shock, which can be extremely serious. If your dog has pale or white gums, is breathing rapidly, or you can see or feel its heart beating very quickly, it could be in shock. By staunching bleeding quickly, this can be avoided.

As with cuts to human skin, a quick way to stop bleeding is to apply pressure. Of course, this will be easier to achieve on some parts of your dog than others. If your dog is actually spouting blood, it will need professional help immediately. For most types of external bleed, however, first aid is quite straightforward to administer.

(For the sake of convenience, we'll assume you are at home and have access to your dog's first aid kit. If you are out and about, you may be able to improvise, or you may decide it's best to call the vet and ask their advice.)

Bleeding from the Head or Torso

To treat bleeding from your dog's head or torso, you will first have to restrain it. Starting with your verbal skills, calm your dog and apply its leash safely. Remember it is at these times that it is most likely to bite. Once you have applied its leash, wrap the rest of it around something solid. The idea is to immobilise your dog's head completely. This will keep you safe and stop the dog from further injuring itself.

Apart from the likely distress it will cause, the main reason to stop bleeding as soon as possible is to prevent shock. If your dog loses enough blood, its nervous system will go into shock, which can be extremely serious.

Once you have your dog's head immobilised, you may want to use its muzzle. Again, this is because it may try and bite you at any time. Once muzzled, you can safely treat the source of your dog's bleeding, as follows:

1 Apply pressure directly to the wound. It should stop bleeding after no more than a couple of minutes.

2 Once bleeding is staunched, cover the wound with fresh gauze pad, clean towel or appropriate sanitary material.

3 Wrap the dressing with soft cloths or other bandage material (see Principles of Bandaging), just tight enough to keep the dressing in place.

4 Take your dog carefully to the vet (see *Transporting Your Dog Safely*).

Bleeding Leg, Paw or Tail

Bleeding from any of these appendages will inevitably cause your dog to lick the affected area, and probably whine. Again, you'll need to restrain your dog safely, using a reassuring voice. Once your dog is calm enough to work with, take the following steps:

1 Clip the hair around the affected area carefully to gain access to the wound.

2 Examine the wound for any objects still in it. This could often be glass, so be careful not to cut yourself or further injure your dog. If you can see a foreign object, remove it as gently as possible with tweezers or your fingers if necessary.

3 Move the skin gently backwards and forwards around the wound. If the wound does not completely move with the skin, it will be deep enough to need stitches.

4 Flush the wound out using clean water. **Do not** apply any antiseptics, as these will be painful for your dog and distress it further. You want your dog as calm as possible while you are applying first aid.

5 Cover the wound with a new gauze pad or another sterile dressing.

6 Put your hand all the way over the dressing and press down firmly.

7 Keep applying pressure to try to stop the bleeding. If blood soaks through the dressing, **Do not** remove it, but add another dressing and continue applying pressure. After 5 minutes, if the bleeding has not stopped, you'll need to go to the veterinary surgery immediately, or call out an emergency vet if you can. In the meantime, keep applying pressure to the wound and adding extra dressings if needed.

8 If only a couple of specks of blood are visible through the top layer of dressing, you have successfully staunched the bleeding. Well done! Now, keep the dressings in place and wrap them with bandage material (see Principles of Bandaging). Start beyond the wound and wrap inwards, don't wind the bandage too tight, and tape in place when you're finished.

9 If you saw that the wound needed stitching, take your dog to the vet and keep it off its injured leg on the way (see *Transporting Your Dog Safely*).

Bleeding Chest or Abdomen

A wound in either of these areas means you will have to restrain your dog safely and apply a muzzle. Once you have done this, examine your dog either on its side, sitting or standing depending where the bleeding is coming from.

1 If the bleeding is coming from the chest area around the rib cage, listen carefully. If you can hear a sucking sound, you need to get your dog to a vet as soon as possible. Put bandaging around your dog over the wound to stop air entering and seek help immediately.

2 If there is no sucking noise, examine the wounded area and look for anything sticking out of your dog. This could be a broken branch or maybe an arrow. If there is anything protruding from your dog's chest or abdomen, again you will have to take it to the vet immediately. **Do not** attempt to remove the object.

a Pad the area around the wound with sterile dressings.

b Bandage around the area tightly to stop the object moving.

c Take your dog to the veterinary surgery as carefully as possible.

3 If there is no sucking noise, and nothing is protruding from your dog's chest or abdomen, clip the hair around the wounded area to gain access.

4 Check for broken glass or other small objects around or in the wound itself. If you see any, carefully remove with tweezers. Move the skin around the wound to see if it requires stitches.

5 Flush the wound out thoroughly using clean water. **Do not** apply antiseptic.

6 Cover the wound with sterile dressings such as new gauze pads or other sanitary material.

7 Place your hand over the dressed area and apply pressure. If blood continues to soak through the dressing, **Do not** remove it, but add further sterile dressings. Keep applying pressure and dressings for 5 minutes. If bleeding has still not stopped, take your dog to the vet, still applying pressure.

8 Once you have staunched the bleeding, wrap it in bandaging material (see Principles of Bandaging). Tape the bandages just tightly enough to keep them in place.

9 If the wound needs stitches, take your dog to the vet as soon as possible (see *Transporting Your Dog Safely*).

Bleeding Ear

> As with humans, dogs' ears tend to bleed profusely. Depending on the breed, dogs' ears can also be quite prone to cuts, due to the animals' inquisitive natures.

As with humans, dogs' ears tend to bleed profusely. Depending on the breed, dogs' ears can also be quite prone to cuts, due to the animals' inquisitive natures. Fortunately, a bleeding ear is one of the easier wounds to treat with first aid.

1 Safely restrain your dog using verbal calming techniques. If you feel safer using a muzzle, apply one before you examine the wound.

2 Taking a sterile dressing or clean cloth, fold it around the edge of your dog's ear where it is bleeding. Apply pressure on both sides of the ear with your fingers and thumb.

3 Fold your dog's ear directly over the top of its head. This will keep it out of sight, and help reduce blood flow. Keep applying pressure on the ear to stem the bleeding.

4 Bandage your dog's entire ear (see *Principles of Bandaging*) in this position.

5 Transport your dog to the vet for immediate attention (see *Transporting Your Dog Safely*).

Bleeding Nails

Dogs' nails usually bleed when they have been cut too short, or have broken against some hazard. If you are not comfortable with clipping your dog's nails, you should take it to a professional dog groomer. If, however, you have cut your dog's nail too short, it could bleed for quite a long time.

1 Safely restrain your dog. You **must** apply a muzzle before attempting first aid on your dog's paw.

2 If your dog has broken a nail, hold a sterile dressing or clean cloth tightly against the bleeding nail. It will stop bleeding after a couple of minutes. Once it has, take your dog straight to the vet, keeping it off the affected paw.

3 If you have cut your dog's nail too short, as well as applying its muzzle, you **must** restrain its head. Use its leash and tie it securely to something heavy so its head is immobile.

4 As with a broken nail, apply a sterile dressing to the bleeding area. Keep the pressure on until the bleeding stops. As a guide, this will probably take at least 5 minutes. **Do not** remove the dressing in the meantime.

5 If the bleeding has not stopped after 15 to 20 minutes, you should take your dog to the veterinary surgery immediately. This kind of bleeding might indicate a blood disorder (see *Transporting Your Dog Safely*).

Internal Bleeding

Unlike external bleeding, if your dog is bleeding internally, it requires emergency treatment whatever the circumstances. Basically, if your dog has internal bleeding, you have an emergency on your hands. Also unlike external bleeding, you may not actually see blood. These are the signs to look for in relation to internal bleeding in your dog:

- Pale or white gums

- Rapid heartbeat and / or breathing

- Bleeding from the ears

- Bleeding from the nose

- Bleeding from the mouth

- Bleeding from the rectum

If you see any of these signs, you need to get your dog to a vet immediately. If your dog has pale or white gums, it is almost certainly in shock. To check:

- Lift your dog's lip gently to check its upper gum line. If the gum is pink, your dog is not in shock. If it is pale or white, you have an emergency.

- Put your finger tips firmly on your dog's rib cage a couple of inches from the elbow of either leg. Count the number of heartbeats in 10 seconds, and multiply by 6. If this comes to more than 150 per minute, your dog could be in shock due to internal bleeding.

After calling the vet, take the following action to treat your dog for shock:

- Lie it on its side with its muzzle pulled slightly upward to keep its airway clear. Gently pull your dog's tongue forward through its mouth.

- Lift your dog's rear end off the floor using a cushion, pillow, folded blanket or towels.

- Wrap your dog in a foil blanket if you have one, or other warm blanket or jacket, to conserve its body heat.

- Transport your dog to the veterinary surgery immediately (see *Transporting Your Dog Safely*).

9

Common Injuries and Illnesses

There are a number of ways in which your dog can suddenly feel ill, or types of injury which most dogs get regularly. The more experience you have of each of those, the easier you will be able to deal with them. Not all require a visit to the vet, so you can have your dog up and running again as soon as possible. Others are more serious, but, as we have seen with some quite challenging scenarios, the right first aid is a fantastic way of giving your dog the best chance of recovery.

Any dog owner will have to face a number of challenges, especially over the many years of a dog's lifetime. Some of the illnesses and injuries which befall them might sound unlikely, but in fact these are the type of things faced by dog owners all the time. If any of them happens to your dog, don't worry; it's nothing that millions of owners haven't faced before.

Seizures

Convulsions, or seizures as they are also known, can be worrying, as they often seem to come out of nowhere. Your dog may never have one, but if it does, try to remember that dogs have seizures all the time, for a number of reasons. Facing your first one will be the hardest.

It may help you to know what a convulsion actually is. It happens when your dog's brain sends a stream of electrical signals to its muscles, in an unusual pattern. All muscles work in response to these signals, but with a convulsion there are too many signals for the muscles to cope with. What happens is that the muscle tissue locks, much like a computer when it is trying to respond to too many commands.

Once your dog's muscles have locked, they will take time to recover their normal functions. This is what happens in the vast majority of cases; there is no permanent damage. In the meantime, of course, watching your dog have a seizure is not pleasant.

Epilepsy is one cause of seizures, but by no means the only one. Other causes of seizures are:

- Poisoning by lead or other substances
- Liver diseases
- Kidney failure
- Brain tumour

> Your dog may never have one, but if it does, try to remember that dogs have seizures all the time, for a number of reasons. Facing your first one will be the hardest.

Obviously, you don't want your dog to be suffering from any of the above. While seizures are common, their causes need to be ascertained as quickly as possible. Any time your dog has a seizure, make sure you take it to the veterinary surgery as soon as possible afterwards.

Seizures usually last a few minutes, after which your dog will be confused and possibly a bit dazed. This will last for between 15 minutes and half an hour. While the seizure itself is actually happening, the biggest risks to your dog's health come from it injuring itself. As it has no control over its muscles, you have to take steps to keep your dog safe.

The most important thing to remember is not to panic. The seizure will stop of its own accord, and you will just have to be patient until it does. In the meantime, these are the essential steps to take:

Do not try to put anything into your dog's mouth. People sometimes have the idea that they should do this to stop the animal from biting its tongue. That is something which may apply to human beings, but you really don't have to worry about it with your dog. What you do have to worry about is getting badly bitten.

Carefully take hold of your dog by whatever parts of its body give you best purchase, ideally its lower legs. Pull it away from any walls or large objects such as furniture, so it doesn't injure itself.

Wrap your dog in a blanket to give it extra protection against injury.

If the seizure lasts for more than 10 minutes, or if your dog has another seizure within an hour, it needs to go to the vet.

Once your dog comes out of its seizure, call your vet while it is recovering. They will give you any further instructions they think appropriate based on what you tell them.

Take your dog to the veterinary surgery. (See our section on *Transporting Your Dog Safely*.)

Stings and Foreign Bodies

Stings

Your dog could suffer from a sting at any time. This can happen as easily in the home as when out and about in the city or the countryside. As with humans, dogs can suffer allergic reactions to stings. If this happens, you need to get your dog to a veterinary surgery as soon as possible. In the mean time, here are some steps you can take to help your dog through the worst of an allergic reaction to a sting:

- If you notice any local swelling (also called urticaria) on your dog's face, paw or leg, this could be the sign of a sting. If you can see a sting in your dog's skin, remove it with tweezers, or your fingers if you can.

- Call the vet, and ask their advice. It could be that giving your dog a Piriton tablet is all that it needs. Be sure to ask for advice first, however.

- If your dog has been stung by a bee, after removing the sting itself, treat the wounded area with a solution of sodium bicarbonate.

- If your dog has been stung by a wasp, rub the area with apple cider vinegar if you have any. The compounds in this vinegar help neutralise the venom in the wasp sting.

- If the sting is on your dog's face or throat area, you need to call a vet quickly. Short nosed dogs especially are vulnerable to facial stings. Take your dog to the vet as soon as possible (see the section on *Transporting Your Dog Safely*).

Foreign Bodies

If your dog gets some kind of foreign body in its eye, it will become distressed. If you notice any distress, and see your dog trying to paw its eye or shake its head violently, it could be trying to rid itself of the object or creature. As the eye is a very sensitive area, these can be painful and worrying for your dog.

Safely restrain your dog, and examine its eyes. If you see a foreign body in either of them, try to remove it. The best way to do this is with slightly salty water, but tap or bottled water will do. Gently try to remove the object by flushing your dog's eye.

If the foreign body has actually penetrated your dog's eye, this is an emergency. **Do not** try to remove the object or creature, but call your vet immediately and try to pacify your dog as much as possible.

If your dog has been unlucky enough to have an eye pop out, you can help by covering it with a water based lubricant, such as KY jelly. Of course, you need to take your dog to the vet immediately. See the section on *Transporting Your Dog Safely*.

Animal Bites

As a lively, inquisitive and intuitive animal, your dog will inevitably encounter other animals on its travels. As well as other dogs, there are plenty of other species roaming round our countryside and cities. As many of these are carnivores, they all have sharp teeth which can give very nasty bites. These are very easy to pick up, and can happen in the blink of an eye, even if your dog is on its leash.

If your dog gets into a fight, whether it's on the leash or not, your first instinct might be to break the fight up. This can be very dangerous. Do not try to break up an animal fight with your bare hands. You may well get bitten, even by your own dog. When dogs fight, they bite anything in their way, so make sure that doesn't include you.

If your dog is on its leash, pull it away from the other animal or animals. You may have to drag it forcefully, but the sooner it's out of harm's way the better. Always keep yourself behind your dog until it is safely away from the fight. If your dog is not on its leash, try to find a big stick or something else long and sturdy. Use it to push or pull your dog away from danger.

> **When dogs fight, they bite anything in their way, so make sure that doesn't include you.**

Checking Wounds

If your dog has been involved in a fight, it's important you check for any wounds. Some of these may be obvious, but your pet may have a number of hidden wounds under its fur. Tooth puncture wounds are common around the neck area, and on the legs. After safely restraining your dog, check its coat for any signs of blood.

After any fight with another animal, but especially a wild one, it's important to think about **Rabies**. Your dog will have been inoculated against this, but others may not have been. If you are not sure of the status of your dog's rabies inoculation, check with your vet immediately. If the other animal is a family pet, find out from its owner the status of its rabies inoculation; however, in the case of a wild animal, strict procedures should be followed.

The only way to check if a wild animal has rabies is for it to be destroyed and have its brain examined by a vet. How you go about this will vary according to circumstances, but remember never to touch a wild animal with your bare hands, even if it's dead. If it is, you'll need to wear gloves and use a blanket to take the animal to the vet's for examination.

Bite Treatments

If your dog has been bitten, these are the steps you should take:

- Apply safe restraint, using a muzzle and immobilising your dog's head. Bite wounds are very painful, and your dog may try to bite you.

- Clip your dog's hair around the bite wound area. Flush the wound thoroughly with clean water, and **do not** use any domestic antiseptics, as these will be very painful on bite wounds.

- Inspect the wound carefully. Use your fingertips to move the skin gently around the bite, to see if the teeth marks are deep enough to require stitches, or your dog's flesh is torn.

- If the wound stops bleeding, **Do not** apply dressings or bandages. It should be left to drain of its own accord.

- If it continues to bleed, try to staunch the bleeding. Put a sterile dressing over the wound and press down hard. If bleeding continues, add another dressing and repeat until bleeding stops.

If you think the wound requires stitches, take your dog to the veterinary surgery immediately (see our section on *Transporting Your Dog Safely*).

Poisoning

While it might sound dramatic, poisoning is something that happens to dogs rather a lot. Unlike with humans, where this is the result of some terrible plot, dogs often poison themselves accidentally. Taking poison basically means eating or drinking something you shouldn't or which is bad for you. Dogs eat and drink an awful lot of things they probably shouldn't. While you can try to keep your dog away from harmful substances, its natural curiosity and extremely sensitive nose will take it to places you just can't control.

This can happen very quickly, even if you have your dog on its leash. There could be poisonous material of any sort hidden in the grass or under leaves. Unfortunately, sometimes the only way you and your dog find out if they are poisonous is after your dog has tried to eat or drink them.

This might happen second hand, or paw, as it were. If your dog steps in something, its nature will be to lick itself clean. It could be carrying round liquids or solids on its paws while out for a walk, and not lick the substance off until it gets home.

Substances Poisonous to Dogs

Dogs can be poisoned by an amazing amount of substances. Unfortunately, a lot of these are kept around the average home. Try to keep your dog away from the following:

- Anything alcoholic
- ammonia
- antifreeze
- bleach
- chocolate (especially baking chocolate)
- detergent
- disinfectant
- dry-cleaning solution
- fertilizer
- furniture polish
- glue
- grapes and raisins
- human medication
- mothballs
- mouse and rat poison
- onions
- oven cleaner
- paint thinner and remover
- petrol
- shoe polish
- silver polish
- toilet bowl cleaner.

If that weren't enough to worry about, many household plants are poisonous to dogs. These include:

- Aloe vera
- amaryllis
- avocado
- azalea
- bird of paradise
- calla lily
- castor bean
- corn plant
- cyclamen
- daffodil
- day lily
- dieffenbachia
- Easter lily
- elephant ears
- English ivy
- gladiolus
- holly
- hyacinth
- hydrangea
- iris

- kalanchoe
- macadamia nut
- mistletoe
- narcissus
- philodendron
- poinsettia

- rhododendron
- tomato plant
- tulip
- yew
- yucca.

Signs of Poisoning

Signs to look for if your dog has been poisoned are:

- Excessive drooling
- Seizures
- Coma
- Vomiting
- Diarrhoea

- Abdominal pain
- Twitching
- Nervousness
- Chemical smell somewhere on the body.

If your dog falls into a coma, or has a seizure after obviously ingesting a poisonous substance, it is best to stay on the safe side and take it to the vet straight away, along with the substance it has ingested. Wrap your dog in a blanket and take it to the veterinary surgery (see the section on Transporting Your Dog Safely).

If you detect a chemical smell anywhere on your dog, you should wash it completely. Use warm, soapy water and bathe or clean your dog's entire coat several times until the smell has completely gone. You may also like to flush out your dog's mouth with clean water in case it has licked itself. Keep an eye out for any signs of poisoning.

You may need to make your dog vomit. This is not always advisable, however. If your dog has ingested any caustic or petroleum based products, **Do not** force it to vomit. Caustic substances include battery acid, corn and callous remover, dishwashing detergent, drain cleaner, grease remover, lye, and oven cleaner. Petroleum based products include paint solvent, floor wax, and dry-cleaning solution.

If your dog falls into a coma, or has a seizure after obviously ingesting a poisonous substance, it is best to stay on the safe side and take it to the vet straight away, along with the substance it has ingested.

If your dog has not already vomited, and you are sure it has not ingested any caustic or petroleum based product, you should induce it to vomit. To do this safely:

Based on your dog's weight, give it one tablespoon of hydrogen peroxide per 20 pounds of weight. Do this every ten minutes until your dog starts to vomit. If it has not vomited after half an hour, take your dog to the veterinary surgery immediately (see the section on Transporting Your Dog Safely).

If you suspect your dog may have ingested anything poisonous to it;

- Contact your local Veterinary Practitioner or Animal Welfare Office.

10

Questions to Ask
When Adopting a Dog

A lot of people would like to adopt a rescue dog, but are uncertain whether it's really a good idea. This is perfectly understandable; in fact, a responsible rescue dog owner should ask questions. What follows is a list of what you should know before, during and after going to the dog shelter.

What's the dog's history?

This is the most commonly asked question, and rightly so. Just as an animal shelter will ask you questions about your own circumstances, so you should ask about your rescue dog's. In fact, it would be irresponsible if you didn't. Don't be afraid to ask as many questions as you want about how the dog came to be rescued, and what sort of life it's had so far. Most dogs will be found as strays, given up by their owners, or rescued after complaints to animal charities. This will affect how much the animal sanctuary knows about the rescue dog.

Has its behaviour been tested?

There are a number of behavioural tests which dog shelters can carry out. These should be done as a matter of course, before dogs are put up for adoption. Some charities or agencies may carry out more thorough tests than others. The first thing to check is that at least some have been done; if not, don't think about adoption. If testing has been carried out, ask for a detailed list of what the tests were, and what the results were. If you have particular concerns for your home, you will want to know your rescue dog is suitable.

What medical attention has the dog had?

Like any dog, a rescue dog will need to have had certain vaccinations by a particular age. The shelter's own veterinary surgeons should be top quality, and be able to tell you the dog's vaccination status, as well as any known illnesses or injuries it has suffered from. Heartworm checks are an absolute necessity, as are rabies vaccinations. You will need to take over the dog's immunisation schedule, so ask if there is anything extra to be taken care of.

What adoption process does the shelter have?

Some dog shelters have more thorough procedures for allowing pets out for adoption than others. You should check what their system is before you visit the agency, to avoid disappointment. In some cases, a dog shelter will let you take a dog away the first time

> Like any dog, a rescue dog will need to have had certain vaccinations by a particular age. The shelter's veterinary surgeons should be top quality, and be able to tell you the dog's vaccination status, as well as any known illnesses or injuries it has suffered from.

you visit, if it thinks you're an appropriate adopter. Other charities and shelters insist on introducing the rescue dog to all family members, including any pets. You may prefer this more thorough approach, but you should check out the shelter's adoption timeline first.

How much will it cost?

Don't expect the animal shelter to have a flat fee for every rescue dog it puts up for adoption. Prices vary between charities or other agencies, and can also depend on the age and breed of the animal. Market forces apply, as dog shelters have to keep themselves solvent as best they can. Young puppies often cost more than older dogs, and certain breeds are more attractive to some owners, therefore will attract a higher fee. Do your research before visiting the shelter.

What is the dog's current diet?

As well as finding out your rescue dog's feeding times, it is also essential to know what food it has been eating. The shelter's vets will have prescribed the type of diet they think best for the type and age of your rescue dog, so this could be an excellent guide for when you get the dog home. Talk to the vet about feeding regimes and the types of food to avoid.

Final Word

Adopting a rescue dog is one of the most rewarding things in many people's lives. For individuals and families, the love which rescue dogs provide can be like no other. Giving a dog a new start in life after some bad experiences can lead to a special bond like no other, which lasts a lifetime. There may be challenges to overcome, to be sure. These can test the commitment of you as an owner, in some quite surprising ways. The early days and weeks provide their own challenges, but longer term issues might be with a dog all its life. Really getting to know a rescue dog as it grows into your family is where the real reward lies.

We hope we have given you some helpful tips, and confidence to proceed with adopting a rescue dog. For the vast majority of adopters, taking the decision to welcome a rescue dog into their home and family is the best choice they ever made. Here's to you and many years of happiness together!

Here are some trusted dog re-homing agencies:

Blue Cross (UK)

American Dog Rescue Foundation (USA)

RSPCA Australia

SPCA New Zealand

ISPCA Ireland